Stuff I've Been Feeling Lately

poetry by:

Alicia Cook

RADIANT SKY
PUBLISHING GROUP

ISBN-13: 978-1522949251
ISBN-10: 1522949259

i

Dedication

This book is dedicated to anyone who loves
someone struggling with addiction.
All royalties earned will be donated directly to
the Willow Tree Center in New Jersey.
www.willowtree.org

And as always, Mom and Dad...
thank you.

-Alicia

side a

The Poems

Track One

This is dedicated to the man who saved me.

> He didn't save me from a car wreck.
> Though my existence managed to swerve
> off the road, creating a mangled mess
> even the Jaws-of-Life couldn't tear through.
>
> He didn't save me from fiery flames.
> Quite the contrary,
> and perhaps even a bit more frightening,
> the fire inside of me had long burned out.
>
> He didn't save me from drowning,
> at least not in the literal sense.
> I can swim just fine;
> but the rip currents of life took me under,
> and I began to flounder in my own tears.

Simply, this is dedicated to the man who saved me
from the biggest catastrophe of all: myself.

Currently Listening To:

Ellie Goulding, "How Long Will I Love You?"

Track Two

You always want one more day.
You always want one more picture
as the old ones begin to fade.
You always want that one final hug
to have lasted just a tad longer.
You always want the fondness
of the "*remember-whens*"
to outnumber the "*might-have-beens*."
You want more years, more months,
more weeks, more days,
more minutes, and more seconds.
You want the "happily ever after"
you always thought you deserved,
but the only thing actually promised
in this life is uncertainty.

Currently Listening To:

Kanye West, "DreamKillers"

Track Three

I comb through my memories
with more care than I do my hair.
I'm told the key is to preserve the root.
Still, I have difficulty remembering things.
I recall second natures in partials,
                              never wholes.

I flip through photo albums
and see my likeness in someone
I can't manage to recognize anymore,
                              even when I squint.

She shares my fingerprints.
They tell me it's me.

It's as if I am wearing hand-me-down memories
from a life that doesn't quite fit right.
They were a gift, so squeeze into them.
I experience that familiar itch of frustration
as I struggle to name the girl in the photo.

Imagine the anguish felt
            by having your very own existence
                  on the tip of your tongue.

Currently Listening To:

Sara Bareilles, "She Used to Be Mine"

Track Four

Yeah, she's beautiful.
  Anyone with decent eyesight can tell you that.
  But that's not why I love her.

I love her when she is putting her make up on,
  sitting on the bathroom counter.

I love her when she makes me order
  the Chinese or pizza but constantly whispers
  the order into my ear because she is convinced
  I'll mess it up.

I love her when we are walking and she trips
  over nothing on the sidewalk and keeps talking,
  not missing a beat, like it just didn't happen.

I love her when we are packing the car for a trip
  and she hands me seven bags.

I love her when she is curled up on our couch
  wearing my shirt.

I love her after her first sip of coffee
  or her last sip of wine.

I love her when she first gets out of the shower
    in the summer and I see her vivid tan lines.

I love her when she steals the covers all night
    and then, come morning,
    blames it on the fact that I turned on the fan.

I love her when we drive around during the holidays,
    her feet up on the dashboard,
    sipping hot chocolate and
    looking at Christmas lights.

Currently Listening To:

Lee Brice, "A Woman Like You"

Track Five

She was a pro at being dependently-happy.
She jumped from one "happiness" to the next
(You're the only one.)
They made her smile
(You're beautiful;)
until they made her cry
(But I'm not looking to settle down.)
>They broke her heart
>*(This isn't working anymore,)*
>and her spirit
>*(But let's still be friends.)*
>>Over and over again
>>she trusted the fragments of her soul
>>with others
>>*(I'd never hurt you like he did.)*
>>She thought they could fix her.
>>>Once they inevitably
>>>abandoned her
>>>*(It's not you, it's me,)*
>>>she would end up leaving
>>>with more of them than of
>>>herself.
>And this how a person's own reflection
can become unrecognizable.

Currently Listening To: O.A.R., "Shattered"

Track Six

The strongest people I know have been
overtaken by their weaknesses.
They know what it's like to lose control.
The strongest people I know have cried
in the shower and in their car.
They know loss and guilt all too well.
The strongest people I know are not bulletproof.
They have felt the searing pain of life's shots.
The strongest people I know make the decision
every day to wake up
and place their two feet on the ground
even though they know the monsters
beneath their bed will grab at their ankles.
The strongest people I know
are not "strong" by definition, at all.

They are mistake-makers.
They are mess-creators.
They are survivors.

Currently Listening To:
50 Cent, "In Da Club"

Track Seven

To Whom It May Concern:

Drive away. You don't live here anymore.

You are not home free if you are still calling this place "home." Check your mirrors. *Images are closer than they appear and not as pretty as they seem.* Those rose-colored sunglasses of yours are playing tricks on your eyes. This nostalgic route is messing with your heart. That familiar song on the radio has penetrated your mind.

Honestly, I hope you don't spend one minute missing me. Missing this. You will heal as long as you don't turn around. Ever. Sometimes even a glance into the past can kill you.

Sincerely,
The Girl You Used To Be.

Currently Listening To:

The Weepies, "Can't Go Back Now"

Track Eight

She lost herself;

I'm talking *down-the-rabbit-hole* freefall like the little blonde girl in that book she read once. She was so far gone that even her own shadow kicked her when she was down. Friends and family would tell her she would be her "old self" in no time flat.

"You'll find yourself again," they would say. They would promise her this in hopes she would find comfort in the possibility. They made it seem like a blessing. To her, the idea of becoming herself again felt more like a curse. Why would she purposely go hunting for that girl just to feel all the pain she had once felt?

Why? If that meant having the memories, mistakes, and regrets find her again, too? No, she didn't want to become her old self again, ever.

If she survived her latest misadventure, she vowed to become someone entirely new.

Currently Listening To:

Rachel Platten, "Fight Song"

Track Nine

The first time my heart broke, I thought back to the day in my childhood when a piece of glass went through my finger after an ill-fated cartwheel.

I was 11-years-old.

My mother and I were in our bathroom cleaning up the wound. She dribbled peroxide onto the cut. It fizzed and burned; I winced at the pain.

"It needs to burn so you know it's healing,"
                                   she explained.

That small exchange during my adolescence helped me learn to appreciate the pain pulsating from my broken heart. That way, in spite of the severity of my wound, I knew the healing process had already begun.

Currently Listening To:

Big Sean, "Dark Sky (Skyscrapers)"

Track Ten

I had become accustomed to using moving boxes as makeshift coffee tables. Never in one place for too long. Always in my car longer than any bed; but there was an anomaly in that last drive.

It was one of those special car rides where every song on the radio was one of my favorites. The road was open and smooth, freshly paved.

And the thing is I wasn't driving anywhere new. For once in my life, home had become a singular destination for me. I regained my soul through you. I had regained my soul through our consistency.

Currently Listening To:

Miranda Lambert, "Making Plans"

Track Eleven

You can taste sorrow in salt tears and in the bitterness
of spoiled words left in your mouth for far too long.
You can hear sorrow in a familiar song.

You can hide sorrow behind closed doors and
inside screams muffled by pillowcases.

You can stick to sorrow as if it were gum in your hair;
too mangled to brush out, too jarring to chop off.
You can see sorrow in bloodshot eyes and shaky
hands.

You can get lost in sorrow when it knocks your life
off course with no detour signs to redirect you.

But
most importantly,
you can be found in sorrow
by becoming a different version of yourself,
here, on the other side of tragedy.

Currently Listening To:

Bright Eyes, "Hit the Switch"

Track Twelve

My "new beginnings" have often spawned from forced endings. With one of life's chapters being ripped from my hands before I even had time to dog-ear my favorite parts. For a very long time I confused the notion of a "fresh start" with walking towards distress instead of away from it.

Now, I relish the thought of
> getting to know the unknown.
> Getting to familiarize myself with the unfamiliar.
> Getting to start over smack dab in the middle of my life.

Currently Listening To:

Craig Mack feat. Notorious B.I.G., LL Cool J, "Flava in Ya Ear (Remix)"

Track Thirteen

There has always been a disconnect
  between me and the world around me.
I never felt settled, grounded.
Suddenly, it became so clear.
Perhaps I lost myself so often because
  I found my sandy feet in a shore town.
All my life, my footprints were repeatedly
  washed away by the tide,
    as if I never existed there in the first place.

Currently Listening To:

Miranda Lambert, "Airstream Song"

Track Fourteen

Just because I don't trust you
       doesn't mean I have trust issues.
Just because I won't commit to you
       doesn't mean I have commitment issues.
Just because I watch what I eat
       doesn't mean I have body image issues.
Just because people have left my life
       doesn't mean I have abandonment issues.
Just because I yearn to grow and evolve
       doesn't mean I have identity issues.

I know exactly who the hell I am.

Currently Listening To:

Chris Brown feat. André 3000, Drake, Fabolous,
Kanye West, T.I., "Deuces"

Track Fifteen

A picture never fully captures
the reasons behind
why we want to document the moment
in the first place.

It doesn't capture the distant smell
of a fireplace burning as it's quickly overtaken
by the unmistakable aroma of low tide.

It doesn't capture the cleansing scent
of salt air entering my nostrils.
It doesn't capture the monstrous howl
of the wind whipping through my hair
or the pleasurable sting of the sand in my eyes.

It doesn't capture the transformation
in the texture of the sand beneath my feet
as I approach the breakers.

It doesn't capture the unexpected warmth
of November's ocean as it reaches my ankles.

The lens of a camera cannot capture any of that;
my heart does.

Currently Listening To: Lady Antebellum,
"Goodbye Town"

Track Sixteen

The "new normal" is rarely an easy adjustment,
and never truly feels, well, "normal."

Let's be honest.

"Plan B" is never preferred.
Detours and alternate routes are never quite as scenic.

The darkness of being gifted a second chance is that
it means something went wrong in the first place.

And yet,
I would rather be thrown a couple surprise curve balls
than never step up to the plate again.

I would rather have a few speed bumps slow me
down, causing me to spill coffee on my dress,
than ever hand someone else the keys to my life.

Currently Listening To:
Goo Goo Dolls, "Rebel Beat"

Track Seventeen

Sometimes you don't realize you are holding yourself
together
                              until you aren't anymore.

Suddenly, you're not the same person
you thought you were just moments before.

                    No.
        You are not "okay." You are not "fine."
                But you will be.

When I say "you will be okay,"
I do not mean you will wake up one day
and be the same person you were before the pain.

                Pain changes a person.

But, you will discover a new version of "you."
One who has experienced the great sadness
that only follows a great loss.
One who knows the value of a good cry.
One who knows that even after
the coldest of winters,
spring will still arrive.

Currently Listening To:

Eminem, "Till I Collapse"

Track Eighteen

We cleanse our palettes as midnight resets our lives.
Clean slates always taste better when they are fizzy.

Currently Listening To:

Frank Sinatra, "The Best is Yet to Come"

Track Nineteen

There are layers to loving me.

In the beginning, I am quite easy to love.
My surface is smooth, my smiles tender.

But as time undresses,
my insides are revealed to be rough and ragged.
It will become awfully difficult to love me.
At times, borderline impossible.

Many have left; for people would rather
see a car accident unfold from afar,
than be the shotgun rider.

Until you.

Only you can see all you see,
know all you know about me,
and still look at me like this.

Currently Listening To:

Bright Eyes, "First Day of My Life"

Track Twenty

My lifelong person.
The man who will help zip my dress every morning.

How do you do it?

How do you fix everything time and time again
just by surviving through the moment with me?

Currently Listening To:

Pearl Jam, "Just Breathe"

Track Twenty-One

If you are lucky enough to have a childhood friend, try your hardest to grow old with them. These friends are a unique, irreplaceable, breed.

These friends lived through curfews and Polaroid pictures with you. These friends know your parents and siblings because they had to call your house first to speak with you.

Those memories are not frozen in time on social media, but live on nonetheless.

Most importantly, they remember the person you were before the world got a hold of you, so they have this crazy ability to love you no matter what.

They are the living, breathing reflection of where you have been. And so, just when you think you've lost yourself for good, they are there to bring you face-to-face with your true self, simply by sharing a cup of coffee with them.

As your world grows and becomes larger and more complicated than your backyard, even if you establish a life elsewhere, I hope your childhood friends remain lifelong allies, because mine have saved my life on more than one occasion.

Currently Listening To:
The Beatles, "With a Little Help from My Friends"

Track Twenty-Two

I didn't just survive this year,
I lived it.

I laughed, I cried, I scribbled things in journals.
My heart broke, but kept ticking.
My passport earned a few new stamps.
I had fancy Saturdays and lazy Sundays.
I dipped my toes in tropical seas.
I hiked mountains and cheated on my diet.
I made my 29th consecutive birthday wish.

Because of this, and so much more,
I will never settle on simply surviving ever again.
I choose to live.

Currently Listening To:

One Republic, "I lived"

Track Twenty-Three

I want you to know, I love you the other 364 days too.

All the commercially popular grand gestures in the world could never compete with the millions of every day little things you have done, and continue to do, for me. You continue to love me when I am, by definition, unlovable. You continue to love me when I don't particularly love myself. You allow me to remain my quirky self in a world that prefers conformity. I can only hope I bring to you the same feeling of completeness and unconditional acceptance that you have given to me. Love isn't about tangible things.

Love has always been about two people.

And since we are only allotted one life per person, I feel undeniably privileged and fortunate to get to spend my one lifetime with you.

Currently Listening To:

Christina Perri, "Miles"

Track Twenty-Four

I didn't wear a jacket on Sunday. First time in months. I woke up and felt…different. Even before I cracked open my windows to allow what definitely resembled a spring breeze to creep through and ruffle the loose papers on my dresser. Even before I heard birds chirping and a seagull cawing overhead. Even before the aroma of freshly ground coffee entered my nostrils, smelling more like a pleasure than a necessity. It was as if my soul had thawed. I felt completely reinvigorated. Instead of wearing one of my 17 pairs of black yoga pants I had been wearing since November, I opted for an olive green maxi dress and a light cardigan. Others felt the change too. I noticed some girls in flip-flops hopscotching through puddles of melting snow. Call it ridiculous, but there was an upswing in my mood, just at the mere promise of spring. Perhaps my decision to nix the jacket was a symbol for change, not just in the weather, but within myself. I caught a glimpse of the girl I had been missing greatly the last couple of months. It was nice to see her again. So Sunday, I sang along with the radio really loud and unapologetically, I drank three mimosas before one o'clock, and I didn't wear a jacket.

Currently Listening To: Kendrick Lamar, "Bitch Don't Kill My Vibe"

Track Twenty-Five

I am never going to be the girl with the perfectly straightened hair or creased clothing. Even at my most put together, I'll look a bit disheveled.

My socks will never match, but no one will notice that except for my lover and airport security. At the most inopportune times, I'll have a run in my stocking or a runny nose.

I'll combine foods even a pregnant woman wouldn't crave. On way more than one occasion, my friends have said out loud, "I would not want to spend one minute in your head."

I was always aware of what I encompassed. I have never tried to conform because I did not feel the pressure to do so *(thanks, Mom!)* Yes, this self-assurance led to my grade school years being a living hell, but even then I recognized that time of my life as "temporary."

I do not fear, nor am I ashamed of, myself.

And as long as I am happy, it is my God given right to be odd. To be my true self.

Currently Listening To: Taylor Swift, "Mean"

Track Twenty-Six

My soul must have a glass bottom,
the way you peer into my depths with such ease.
You embrace my complexity
and bravely swim against my current.

You do not fear the pull of my murky undertow.
You vow "forever" to me as if it were as simple as
slipping a ring upon my finger…
…because, maybe this time, it is.

Currently Listening To:

Ed Sheeran, "Tenerife Sea"

Track Twenty-Seven

Sometimes it hurts to breathe.
All my corrupt decisions weigh on my chest,
methodically pushing down to crack each rib,
in hopes of infiltrating my heart and finally
exterminating
the last shred of the human being I once was.

If that happens,
if my sanctuary is breached,
I will not stand a chance.

I will lose the one last single atom
that makes me, me.

I can't lose me.
I'm all I've got.

Currently Listening To:

Tupac, "Keep Ya Head Up"

Track Twenty-Eight

Growing up, my mother cautioned I would not possess the power to plan out my life. I couldn't say "I'll be married by X, have a kid by Y, have a book out by Z." I was told as much as I crave to treat my life as one big to-do list, I would instead find myself asking, "where from here?" at least a few times in my life.

Now, I catch myself asking this a few times a day.

"Where from here?"

Three pint-sized words shouldn't be able to pose such a fatal and final question, but alas, they do. If you go right, you can't go left. Even if you backpedal to take the other route just a second later, your fate will already be altered. It's this or that, never both. It is a hard pill for me to swallow, but I do believe it is in the navigation that you find your way, and inevitably find yourself.

Currently Listening To:

Miranda Lambert, "Mama I'm Alright"

Track Twenty-Nine

I carry you with me all of the time,
but I feel your absence most on those days
when I'm the happiest.

Not when I need you the most,
but when I want you here the most.

I believe grief is like a shadow.
It's always there, following you everywhere you go,
but you only see it when the sun is shining on a
beautiful day.

Currently Listening To:

The Band Perry, "If I Die Young"

Track Thirty

A change in the season
always ignited a change
in your heart.

I became angry
with the universe
and its natural
transitions.

I came to fear
our altered rhythm;
the subtle shifts
in both your affection
and in the air.

Seasons
have patterns.
You'd
be back.

And like Winter's
losing fight
against Spring,
I'd thaw.

Currently Listening To:

Griffin House, "Tell Me a Lie"

Track Thirty-One

The ride to the airport is always too short.

Even if I'm packed for days, I'm never ready to go. A nervous feeling inhabits my stomach right before my feet hit the hectic curb.

I check my bag and then head up to security. The line is long as the employee asks, "Are you alone?" *(In life or just right now?)*

He points me in the direction away from the lovers and families traveling together.

The person in front of me doesn't have to remove their shoes but I do *(of course)* so now I'm barefoot in Newark Airport.

I make it to the gate and immediately insert my headphones.

That doesn't stop the Chatty Cathy beside me from asking, "So, where are you coming from?" *(Don't you mean, "What are you running from?")*

Pretending she startled me, I remove my headphones. She repeats the question.

(How specific do you want me to get? I'm coming from therapy. I'm coming from a weekend of binge drinking. I'm coming from a sleepless night due to a migraine I'm still feeling.)

I answer, "New Jersey." She is silent as my headphones go back in.

I've always preferred the more hopeful question, "Where are you heading?"

My answer? *"Everywhere."*

Currently Listening To:

Brand New, "Okay I Believe You but My Tommy Gun Don't"

Track Thirty-Two

There have been nights
I've shared a twin bed with him
and still couldn't get close enough.

Then there have been nights
spent in a king bed where I've felt as though
his annoying ass was still in my personal space.

We e b b and f l o w.

But there's no one else
I'd rather crash into every night
when the tide hits its inevitable peak.

Currently Listening To:

Beyoncé, "Countdown"

Track Thirty-Three

I feel at peace the nights
I find myself naked beneath our sheets;
staring at the ceiling and creating
my own constellations from its paint cracks.

Feeling more connected to the universe in the
moments we spend together under our artificial
plaster sky, than I ever could
on evenings spent outside,
staring up at the starry night sky,
counting actual constellations without you.

Currently Listening To:

Andrew McMahon in the Wilderness,
"Cecilia and the Satellite"

Track Thirty-Four

Not laughing for fear of crying.
Not loving for fear of heartbreak.
Not choosing for fear of wrong decisions.
Not dreaming for fear of nightmares.
Not trusting for fear of betrayal.
Not jumping for fear of broken bones.
Not exploring for fear of getting lost.

Not attempting for fear of failing
is like not living for fear of dying.

It is impossible to escape this world unscathed.
So, embrace this messy, uncertain existence

and

live.

Currently Listening To:

Kacey Musgraves, "Somebody to Love"

Track Thirty-Five

I'm not the one who got away.

Late nights and loneliness have built me up in your head. Letting go of even the wrong heart can play tricks on one's mind, confusing two souls that once mated for soulmates.

So, please, the next time the smell of Chanel fills up a room, and you find yourself reminded of me, try to remember:

I never even wore perfume.

Currently Listening To:

Nancy Sinatra, "Bang Bang"

Track Thirty-Six

I find comfort
in the colors of a sunset.
I find a special magic
in the fact
it never photographs
as beautifully as my eyes
can witness it firsthand.

I find a certain peace
in the conclusion of
another day lived.
And I find hope
in the precarious promise
of tomorrow.

Currently Listening To:

Lee Ann Womack, "I Hope You Dance"

Four children sit together in a room, forming a square.

In the center is a deck of cards. Brand new. Together, using all 52, they construct a house of cards.

They revel at their masterpiece for all of two minutes, as one of their mothers enters the room. Believing it to be muggy, she opens the window.

A gust of wind enters and blows the cards in different directions.

Annoyed a tornado destroyed their work in mere seconds, one child storms out of the room, leaving the door open.

The three remaining children decide to start over.

Card by card the house is reassembled. Immediately following, the family's puppy charges into the room through the opened door and plows into the house of cards like a wrecking ball through cement.

Another one of the children runs out in tears.

The remaining two children recollect the 52 cards and begin to form the foundation once again.

And just as the final card is placed on top, the mother reappears and swings the playroom door closed.

Though brief, the sudden, manufactured airstream causes the house to collapse for the third time just as the door slams shut.

This setback causes another child to march out of the room.

A single child begins gathering the cards.

Her mother comes in and asks why she is playing alone when all her friends are outside. Without even a hesitation, the child responds,

"If I still have the pieces, why wouldn't I keep rebuilding?"

Currently Listening To:
Eminem, "Solider"

Track Thirty-Eight

No matter how old I become, a slight sadness always
washes over me moments before I drive away from
the home where I grew up.

Feelings of melancholy enter the pit of my stomach as
though I am saying goodbye to a dear friend. I stand
at the curb soaking in the last moments of hearing
mother's wind chimes sway in the autumnal air.

It is likely I will live in a few different houses
throughout my life, but I believe there will always
only be one "home" for me.

A home where memories have seeped deep into the
paint and pillows; where unconditional love travels
around the house as if it were another member of the
family.

A sanctuary where pictures, unchanged for years,
hang on the wall as reminders of who I used to be
and how far I have come.

There is something different about the breeze that
passes through the windows of my parent's home; it
somehow holds the power to wrap around me and
rock me until I drift off to sleep.

That cozy security felt by sharing a bedroom wall with my sister. There's something reassuring about seeing my mother's purse slung over a kitchen chair, or my father's shoes by the front door.

In a world where so many unfamiliar variables can arise out of nowhere, it is a comfort to have a very familiar constant.

Home: where love and support concurrently grounded me and encouraged me to fly.

Currently Listening To:

Carrie Underwood, "Don't Forget to Remember Me"

Track Thirty-Nine

This past summer, I was running errands the day I received the worst news of my life. I got the phone call in Target's parking lot, hung up, got out of my car, puked on the side of my tire, and still walked into the store to buy the birthday card I needed.

Now, in the past, I have cried hysterically from happiness. I have laughed uncontrollably out of immense anger. And I have been so overly tired that I was unable to sleep.

But as the red-vested cashier asked the usual, "How are you today?"

I responded, "Fine. Thanks."

And somehow

I think I even managed to smile.

Currently Listening To:
Twenty One Pilots, "Stressed Out"

Track Forty

There are days I spill coffee all over the passenger seat before 7am.

Days I forget to pay bills or respond to wedding invitations.

Days I am overwhelmingly sad for reasons I cannot pinpoint.

Days I will no doubt attempt to pull a door clearly marked "push."

Most days I find myself stumbling over flat surfaces and expectations.

Yet, I know you will love me the same,
and that alone makes my daily missteps less catastrophic.

Eternally Grateful,

Your Hot Mess.

Currently Listening To:

Sublime, "Waiting for my Ruca"

Track Forty-One

A message from the universe appeared in the form of a handwritten note taped to the wall of a nail salon.

"We are not responsible for your loss."

I knew the makeshift sign simply forewarned if I left behind one of my possessions it was my fault, not theirs. Yet, I took it to mean more, as if the world was shaking me awake.

I need to stop making excuses.

I need to stop placing blame. I need to stop renaming the decisions I've made "mistakes" just because I wish I could take them back.

Currently Listening To:

Jay Z feat. Justin Timberlake, "Holy Grail"

Track Forty-Two

I never wanted to help you with your problems
    because I am selfish.

I knew if I were to let you go,
    that alone would solve
    every single issue in your life,
    and I just wasn't ready to leave you yet.

Currently Listening To:

Rita Ora, "Been Lying"

Track Forty-Three

"See you later, Cuz."

These were the last words my cousin ever said to me.

Last words.
What an unusual concept.
We rarely know they are the last as they leave lips.

Our conversation leading up to our goodbye has remained mostly private, just between us two. Though it was a dark time, I am certain she believed in her last words to me. I am certain she believed there would be another day.

Her last words were a promise. And though, yes, we will never see each other again in the physical, I do believe I see my cousin all around me.

In dusty Emerson books and in old Broadway ticket stubs.

In magazines we used to thumb through.

In her mother's laugh. In an eye roll after hearing her father's latest joke.

In a drive by a lake. In yellowed photographs.

In the steep hill of her front lawn.

In shopping for CDs and cheesy Sandra Bullock movies.

In ponytails and black hoodies.

In the title song from "Rent."

In sushi dinners in New York City.

In Christmas mornings and sarcastic remarks.

In an order of buffalo fries, *(extra spicy.)*

In Goo Goo Dolls song lyrics.

And most importantly, in my heart.

I use my words as a vessel to reach her. To stay connected to her. To keep her connected to us. To hold up my end of our promise.

I will see you later, Cuz.

Currently Listening To:
Dr. Dre, "The Message"

Track Forty-Four

The sand beneath my feet
   belongs to September now.
The salt air I breathe
   belongs to September now.
The crashing waves
   belong to September now.

August can have my yesterdays;
   my tomorrows belong
   to September now.

And my heart,
   it belongs to September now, too.

Currently Listening To:

Don Henley, "The Boys of Summer"

Track Forty-Five

Sisters can have very little in common. No shared interests or friends or aspirations. The most my sister and I have in common most days are our blue eyes, parents and my clothes.

Yet, we are tethered together, unfailingly.

It's one thing to have a support system in your life to cheer you on during the instances when everyone is rooting for you. However, it's another thing entirely to look back in your darkest moments and still see them standing in your corner, encouraging you to stay in the ring and FIGHT, when the odds aren't in your favor and all you want to do is throw in the towel.

Not many people in this life will be on your side even when they aren't on your side. Even less who momentarily will slam doors out of frustration, but never actually lock you out.

Unconditional love; that's the definition of "sister."

Currently Listening To:
Irving Berlin, "Sisters, Sisters"

Track Forty-Six

Packing up your belongings means nothing
if you can't box up your heart,
scribble "fragile" along the side,
and take it with you too.

It's hard to walk away, even if you know in your heart
of hearts it's necessary. Even if your feet can't do the
job and you find yourself crawling on your hands and
knees away from a toxic situation,

     be proud of yourself.

You are removing yourself to better yourself
and you will stand on your own two feet again
eventually.

    So crawl, walk, or run,
       the "how" doesn't matter.

Your new life is waiting for you.

Currently Listening To:

    Eric Church, "Give Me Back My Hometown"

Track Forty-Seven

This drugstore lipstick
> is doing a poor job at covering
> my chapped, bitten lips.

My sunglasses
> are doing their best to hide
> the dark circles surrounding my light eyes.

Would the wind feel this cold today if you were still here?

I think back to the last real day we spent together;
> there was nothing special about it.
It was rushed, and I remember the coffee tasting
bitter.
> It's only special now because it was our last.

Though I wish we had traded everlasting last words,
> we didn't. And we won't.

However, now when I have a cup of bad coffee,
it will taste less bitter and more sweet. I will smile and
savor it, like the last real day we shared together.

Currently Listening To:

Lea Michele, "If You Say So"

Track Forty-Eight

I was the kind of kid who would step on ants and then ask my mother if their family would miss them.

When I was 10, I begged my parents for a typewriter and then had my father show me how to draft a professional resume.

When I was 11, I coerced my siblings and cousins to "act" in skits and lip-sync in music videos I filmed with the family camcorder.

When I was 13, I would spend hours after school writing original stories using the characters from Buffy the Vampire Slayer and the members of the Backstreet Boys. I had no idea it was called "fanfiction" at the time.

I was a witch for Halloween six times; not because I lacked creativity, but because I desperately wanted to be a witch. Like, for real.

One day, my uncle looked at me and said, "You're a lonely soul, man." It's possible, I suppose.

I studied English in a Catholic women's college and, for my Senior Thesis, re-wrote Alice in Wonderland from the White Rabbit's perspective. I also explored in writing the idea of Anna Karenina being pushed under the carriage of that passing train against her will.

My professor told me I didn't listen to the essay instructions.

I got the paper back and saw that I earned an "A" anyway with a note saying, "Alicia, though you blatantly ignored the prompt, after reading this succinct conspiracy theory, I can see the original essay topic would have bored you. Does your brain ever slow down?"

Currently Listening To:

Cage the Elephant, "In One Ear"

Track Forty-Nine

I love the way your tongue curls when you are about to sneeze. I love that you don't sit on the same side of the booth as me when we are out to dinner. I love how you pretend to notice my manicure.

And I love that I cannot define the word "love" without saying your name.

Anytime I am anywhere, I wish you were beside me because I am unable to separate my life from yours.

Which leads me to believe

you are my life,

and my life is you;

they are one and the same.

Currently Listening To:

Cast of Wicked, "For Good"

Track Fifty

The shore is always forgiving of the sea,
though they merge together time and time again only
to part.

The sea always returns to kiss the shore,
for both hold the innate understanding that
one cannot exist without the other.

We forgive each other for the very same reason.

Currently Listening To:

Emeli Sande, "Read All About It (Part III)"

side b

The Remixes

Track One

save me

from

drowning

in my own tears.

save me
from myself.

Currently Listening To:

The Fray, "How to Save a Life"

Track Two

You ███ want ████████
████████████████████
█████████████████ ███
████████████████████
██████ a ████████████
████████████████████
████████████ ████████
██████████████████ ██
██████████████████ ██
███████████ █████████
██████████ second ███
█████ "happily ever after"
████████████████████
████████████ ████████
in ██ life ████████

Currently Listening To:

Frank Sinatra's version of
"The Second Time Around"

Track Three

through

difficult   things

I

recognize

life   s

a gift

Currently Listening To:

Drake, "You & the 6"

Track Four

with you

i t

is

like

we are

on

a

████████████████████

████ summer ████████████████

████████████████████
█████████████
████████████████████

████████ drive ████ during ██████████ .
█████████████████
██████████████
██████ Christmas ████

Currently Listening To:

Bing Crosby, "White Christmas"

Track Five

her heart

inevitably

abandoned her

Track Six

weaknesses

a   re

The strongest

monsters

I know

They are mess-creators.

Currently Listening To:

8 Mile Motion Picture, "Final Battle"

Track Seven

You are ██████████████████████
██ m ████████ y ████████████
████████████████████████████
████████████████████████████
████████████████████████████
familiar song ██████████████

██████ ████████████████████████
████████████████████████████
████████████████████████████
██████████

██████████
██████████████████

Currently Listening To:

The Airborne Toxic Event,
"Sometime Around Midnight"

Track Eight

█████████

███████████████

█████████ book s ████████████

███████████████████

███ h ██ old █████████

█████████ the █████████

████ promise ████████████ o █ f █

████████████████████

████████████████████

████████████████████

███████

████████████████

████████████████████

████████████████

████████ adventure ████████

████████████ .

Currently Listening To:

Passenger, "Scare Away the Dark"

Track Nine

███████████████████ I █████████████████

██████████████████████████████

████████████████████████

▌ was ██████████

████████████████████ ████████████

█████████████████████████

████████████████████

██████████████████████

              ████████████████

████████████████████████████

██████████████████████████

broken ███████████████████████

█████████████████████ already ██████

Currently Listening To:

Melanie Safka, "Look What They've
Done to My Song, Ma"

Track Ten

coffee

i   s

one of my favorite

thing s

in   life

The Verve, "Bitter Sweet Symphony"

Track Eleven

a   bitter

song

can hide sorrow

too

Currently Listening To: Amy Winehouse, "Tears Dry on Their Own"

Track Twelve

For a very long time I

wa   s

unknown.

Currently Listening To:

Alessia Cara, "Here"

Track Thirteen

██████████████████████

████████████████████████████

I never ███ settled ██████████

████████████████████

████████████████████████████

████████████ in ██████████

All my life █████████████████████

████████████████████

████████████████████████████

Currently Listening To:

Kacey Musgraves, "Good Ol' Boys Club"

Track Fourteen

████████ I don't ██████
███████ mean ████████████
████████████████ to ██
███████████████████████████
████████████████████
████████████████████████
██████████████████████
████████████ ████████████████
███ cause ███████████████
████████████████████████

███████████████████ hell ████

Currently Listening To:

The Strokes, "Reptilia"

Track Fifteen

██████████████████████

████████████████

███████████████████████

███████████

██████████████████████

██████ b █████████ l ██████

█ u ██████ e ████ ███████

███████████████████

██████████████

███████████████████

███████████████████

████████████████████ eyes

██████████████████

████████████████████

███████████

██████ ca █████ n ███████

███████████████████████.

████████████████ capture ████████

my heart ███.

Currently Listening To:

Snow Patrol, "Just Say Yes"

Track Sixteen

he ███████████ is rarely ████████████
███████████████████████

████ honest

████████████████████
████ and ███████████████████████

████████████████████████████████
████████████████████████████

███ yet,
I ████████████████████████████
████ never ███████████████████

█ w ████ a ████████████████████
████ n ███████ t █████████████
████████████ someone else ████████████

Currently Listening To:

The Growlers, "Naked Kids"

Track Seventeen

████████████████ you are holding yourself
together

████████████████

████████████████
████████ just ████████

██

████████████████ fine.█

████████

████████ you will be okay█
████████████ one day
████████████████████

████████

████████████████████
████████████████
████████████
████████████████
████████████
████████████
████████

Currently Listening To:
Lana Del Rey, "Radio"

Track Eighteen

We clean ███ u█ p████████████████████ our lives.
████████████████████████████████████

Currently Listening To:

Rufus Wainwright, "Hallelujah"

Track Nineteen

██████████████████████

██████████ I am quite ██████████
██████████████████████

████████████
██████████████████████████
████████████████████████
████████████ impossible

███████████████████████
█████████████████████
████████████████████

█████████

██████████████████
██████████████████
██████████████████.

Currently Listening To:

Lenka, "The Show"

Track Twenty

████████████

████████████ will ████████████████████████████

███ *you* ████

████████████████████████████████████
████ surviv ██████████████████ e ██ with me?

Currently Listening To:

Matt Kearny, "Ships in the Night"

Track Twenty-One

memories are

important , they

establish   your

life   ,   mine

have saved m e   .

Currently Listening To:

Tim McGraw feat. Faith Hill,
"Meanwhile Back at Mama's"

Track Twenty-Two

██████████████ this year█
██████

████████████████████████████
██████ broke████████████
███████████████████████
████████████████████████
██████████████████
███████████████████████
█ m██ e█████████████

B██ u███ t████████████
I will never settle ████████████████
██████████.

Currently Listening To:

Zac Brown band, "Highway 20 Ride"

Track Twenty-Three

I want you to ██████████████████████
██

███████████████████████████████
█████████████████████████████████████
██████████████████████████████████
████████████████ love ███████████████
███████████████████████████████████
█████████████ my ██████████████████
████████ quirk █ s ███████████████████
██████████████████████ █ you ████████
█████ complete █████████████████████
████████████ me. █████████████████
███

██████████████████████████████

████████████████████████████████
██████████████████████████████████
█████████████████████

Currently Listening To:

Ingrid Michaelson, "The Way I Am"

Track Twenty-Four

h   e

resembled a spring breeze

and

my soul   thawed. I

w a s

melting snow.

he   promise

d

change,

So   , I sang along with

h

im

.

Currently Listening To:

O.A.R., "Peace"

Track Twenty-Five

I am ▮▮▮ going to be the ▮▮▮▮▮▮▮▮
▮▮▮▮▮▮▮▮▮▮▮▮▮▮▮▮▮▮
▮▮▮▮▮▮▮▮▮▮▮▮▮▮

▮▮▮▮▮▮▮▮▮▮▮▮▮▮▮▮▮▮
▮▮▮▮▮▮▮▮▮▮▮▮▮▮▮▮▮▮
▮▮▮▮▮▮▮▮▮▮▮▮▮▮▮▮▮▮
▮▮▮▮

▮▮▮▮▮▮▮▮▮▮▮▮ woman ▮▮▮
▮▮▮▮▮▮▮▮▮▮▮▮▮▮▮▮
▮▮▮▮▮▮▮▮▮▮▮▮▮▮▮▮
▮▮▮ you ▮▮▮

▮▮▮▮▮▮▮▮▮▮▮▮▮▮▮▮
▮▮▮▮▮▮▮▮▮▮▮▮▮▮▮▮
▮▮▮▮▮▮▮▮▮▮▮▮▮▮
▮▮▮▮▮▮▮▮▮▮▮▮▮▮▮▮
▮▮▮▮▮▮▮▮▮▮▮▮▮▮▮▮▮
▮▮▮▮

▮▮▮ fear, ▮▮▮▮▮▮▮▮▮

▮▮▮▮▮▮▮▮▮▮▮▮▮▮▮▮
▮▮▮▮▮▮ my true self.

Currently Listening To: Frank Sinatra, "My Way"

Track Twenty-Six

My soul ███████████████
██████████ i ███████ s █████████
███████████████
███ brave ████████████

You ████ fear ████████████
█████████████ me █████████████
██████████████
███████████ this time ███ .

Currently Listening To:

Big Sean, "IDFWU"

Track Twenty-Seven

time hurts

human being s.

my
will

i s

all I've got.

The Killers, "All These Things That I've Done"

Track Twenty-Eight

I married

fat e an d will inevitably find you

Currently Listening To:

Dean Martin, "You Belong to Me"

Track Twenty-Nine

██████████████████████████

██ I feel you ████████████████████

████████████████.

███████████████████████

████████████ you ██████████████

████████████████████████

██ a █████ re █████████████████████

████████████████████████████████

beautiful ████

Currently Listening To:

Aayliah, "I Don't Wanna"

Track Thirty

A change ███████

███████████████

in your heart

█████████

█████ i █ s █

a ███ natural

█████

██████ fear

████████████

████████

██████████████

and █████

█████

██████████

████

█████

A ██████████

losing fight

██████████

█████

Currently Listening To: Doris Day, "Que Sera, Sera (Whatever Will Be, Will Be)"

Track Thirty-One

I'm never ready to ▮▮▮

be ▮▮▮

alone ▮▮▮

from ▮ lovers

so ▮▮▮

where are you ▮▮▮ ?

I ▮▮▮

████████████████████████████

████████████████████████████

██████████████████

████ Ne █ e █████████
█ d ████████████

███████████████████████

██████ you ████████

███████████████

Currently Listening To:

Gavin DeGraw, "Still Not Over You"

Track Thirty-Two

████████ nights

██ shared ████████ with him

████████████████

████████ have been ████

████████████████████

████████████████ personal ████.

████████████

██ there's no one else

████████████████

████████████████████.

Currently Listening To:

Fort Minor, "Where'd You Go?"

Track Thirty-Three

████████ the nights
████████████████████
████████ a███ re███
██████████████████████

██████████████████████████
████████████████████ artificial
██████████████████
██████████████
████████████████
████████████████ without you.

Currently Listening To:

Kurt Cobain's cover of
"Where Did You Sleep Last Night?"

Track Thirty-Four

getting lost

is impossible to escape

Currently Listening To:

Missy Higgins, "Where I Stood"

Track Thirty-Five

I █████████████████████

███████████████████████
██ Let ██ go of ██ the wrong heart ████
███████████████████ t █ o ███████████
████████████████

█████████████████████████
███████████ find you ████████████████
████████████

███████████████████████

Currently Listening To:

Mumford & Sons, "Awake My Soul"

Track Thirty-Six

I find a special magic

in

Currently Listening To:

Billy Joel, "For the Longest Time"

Track Thirty-Seven

Four

three

two

on e

collapse

an d

rebuild

Currently Listening To:

Sara Evans, "A Little Bit Stronger"

Track Thirty-Eight

No matter how old I become ██████████ ██████████ ██████████ ██████████

██████████ ██████████ I ██████ ██████████ ██████████ ██████████

██████ will ██████████ ██████████ believe ██████████ ██████████

██████████ in ██ ██████████ unconditional love ████ ██████ as ████████ ██

██████████ ██████████ ██████████

██████████ h █ e ████ holds ██████████ me ██ ████████

he 's

my

world

Currently Listening To:

Jason Mraz, "Won't Give Up"

Track Thirty-Nine

I was running

from

happiness.

n

ow

I   smile.

Currently Listening To:

Snowpatrol, "Run"

Track Forty

██████████████████████

██ before ██

██ I forget to ████████

████ s█

██ay████████████████

███ i█ t

███ I ████████████████

████████

████████████████████████

████████

████████ love ████████

████████████████████

████████

████████████

You ████████

Coldplay, "The Scientist"

Track Forty-One

the universe

knew the

excuses

I

made

Currently Listening To:

Ryn Weaver, "Promises"

Track Forty-Two

I never want ████████████████████████
████████████████████

████████████████ you █

████████████████

████████████████████

████████████████ to leave ████ .

Currently Listening To:

Sugarland, "Stay"

Track Forty-Three

█ you █

█ were █

█

█ an unusual concept

█

█ to █

█

█ me. █

█

█ we

█

█

█

█

█

█

█

█

████████████████████████

█████████████████████████████████
███

████████████████████

███████████████████

█████████████████████

██████████████████████████

████████████████████████

███████████████████

█████████████████████

███████████████████████████ stay
connected to ██████████████████████████
█████████████ our promise.

███████████████

Currently Listening To:

Selena Gomez, "The Heart Wants What it Wants"

Track Forty-Four

████████████████

belong █ to ████████████

██████████████

████████████████

████████████

████████████████

████████████████

████████████████

██████████████

█ my heart

████████████████.

Currently Listening

The Beach Boys, "Wouldn't it Be Nice"

Track Forty-Five

██████████████████████████████████

██████████████████████████████████ my ███

██████████████████████████████████████

████████████████████

████████████████████████████████

████████████████ support system ████████████

████████████████████████████████████ is

rooting for ████████████████████████████████

████████████████████████████████████

██████████████████████████████████████

██████████████████████████████████████

██████████████████████████████████

██

██████████████████████████████

██me ████████████████████████████████████

████████████████████████

████████████████████████████████████

Currently Listening To:

Kanye West, Jay Z, Big Sean, "Clique"

Track Forty-Six

█████████████████████

▌you can████████████

███████████████

█████████████

█████ walk away, ████████████ in your heart

████████████ ██████████████

█ and █████████ ███ on your █████████

███████████████

██████████

████████████████████

██████████████████████ feet ███

█████ .

███████████

███████████████

Your ███ life is waiting ████ .

Currently Listening To:

Notorious B.I.G., "Juicy"

Track Forty-Seven

i ███████████████
    █ do ███████████
  my ████████████████

████████████████
          ██████████ best to ███
████████████████████████████████

████████████████████████████████████

██████████████████████████████████
      ███████████████████████████
███████ remember the ████████████
███
          ████████████████████████ last
████████████████████████ words
we didn't ██████████████

████████████████████████████████
████████████████████████████████
███████████████████ share ████████.

Currently Listening To:

Plain White T's, "Radios in Heaven"

Track Forty-Eight

I was ▮ kind ▮▮▮▮▮▮▮▮▮▮▮▮▮▮▮▮▮▮▮▮
▮▮▮▮▮▮▮▮▮▮▮▮▮▮▮▮▮▮▮▮▮▮▮▮▮▮▮

▮▮▮▮▮▮▮▮▮▮▮▮▮▮▮▮▮▮▮▮▮▮▮▮▮▮
▮▮▮▮▮▮▮▮▮▮▮▮▮▮▮▮▮ to ▮▮▮▮
▮▮▮▮▮▮▮▮▮▮▮

▮▮▮▮▮▮▮▮▮▮▮▮▮ y ▮▮▮▮▮▮ ou ▮▮
▮▮▮▮▮▮▮▮▮▮▮▮▮▮▮▮▮▮▮▮▮▮▮▮
▮▮▮▮▮▮▮▮▮▮▮

▮▮▮▮▮▮▮▮▮▮▮▮▮▮▮▮▮▮▮▮▮▮
▮▮▮▮▮▮▮▮▮▮▮▮▮▮▮▮▮▮▮▮▮▮
▮▮▮▮▮▮▮▮▮▮▮▮▮▮▮▮▮▮▮▮▮▮
▮▮▮▮▮▮▮▮▮▮▮▮▮▮▮▮▮▮
▮▮▮▮▮▮▮▮▮

▮▮▮▮▮▮▮▮▮▮▮▮▮▮▮▮ because I
▮▮▮▮▮▮▮▮▮▮▮ desperately wanted ▮
▮▮▮▮▮▮▮▮▮

▮▮▮▮▮▮▮▮▮▮▮▮▮▮▮▮ You ▮
▮▮▮▮▮▮▮▮▮▮▮▮▮▮

▮▮▮▮▮▮▮▮▮▮▮▮▮▮▮▮ ▮
▮▮▮▮▮▮▮▮▮▮▮▮▮▮▮▮
▮▮▮▮▮▮▮▮▮▮▮▮▮ or ▮

the idea of ███████████

███████████████████████████

█

███████████████████████████

████████

███████████████████████

████████████████████ you

█████████████████████

███████████████████████████

█████████████████████

███████

Currently Listening To:

Bobby Brown, "My Prerogative"

Track Forty-Nine

I love the way ████████████████████████
███████████████████████████████████
██████████████████████████████████
████ you pretend to notice █████████

███████████████████████████████████
████████████████████

██████████████████████████████████ me
███████████████████████████████████

███████████████████

████████████████

████████████████

███████████████████

Currently Listening To:

A Fine Frenzy, "Almost Lover"

Track Fifty

always forgiv███████e

███████ and ██████

return to ██████

each other ██████

Currently Listening To:

Luther Vandross, "I'd Rather"

RADIANT SKY
PUBLISHING GROUP